Collected Poems

Emily Dickinson

About The Author

Emily Dickinson (1830–1886) was an American poet known for her unique and innovative style. Often reclusive, she spent much of her life in her family home in Amherst, Massachusetts. Dickinson's poetry is characterized by its unconventional use of punctuation, slant rhyme, and profound exploration of themes like nature, death, and immortality. Although only a handful of her nearly 1,800 poems were published during her lifetime, she is now considered one of the most significant figures in American literature, influencing countless writers with her introspective and visionary work.

Collected Poems

by Emily Dickinson

Published by Jollyjoy Books Pvt Ltd.

4771/23, Bharat Ram Road, Daryaganj,

New Delhi-110002

E-mail: jollyjoybooks@gmail.com

ISBN: 978-93-6849-709-7

Cover, Typesetting, and Book Design by JollyJoy Books

Contents

1. A Little Road Not Made of Man

A little road not made of man,
Enabled of the eye,
Accessible to thill of bee,
Or cart of butterfly.

If town it has, beyond itself,
'T is that I cannot say;
I only sigh, no vehicle
Bears me along that way.

2. A Wounded Deer Leaps Highest

A wounded deer leaps highest,
I've heard the hunter tell;
'T is but the ecstasy of death,
And then the brake is still.

The smitten rock that gushes,
The trampled steel that springs;
A cheek is always redder
Just where the hectic stings!

Mirth is the mail of anguish,
In which it cautions arm,
Lest anybody spy the blood
And "You're hurt" exclaim!

3. Alter? When The Hills Do

Alter? When the hills do.
Falter? When the sun
Question if his glory
Be the perfect one.

Surfeit? When the daffodil
Doth of the dew:
Even as herself, O friend!
I will of you!

4. Angels In the Early Morning

Angels in the early morning
May be seen the dews among,
Stooping, plucking, smiling, flying:
Do the buds to them belong?

Angels when the sun is hottest
May be seen the sands among,
Stooping, plucking, sighing, flying;
Parched the flowers they bear along.

5. As Children Bid The Guest Good-Night

As children bid the guest good-night,
And then reluctant turn,
My flowers raise their pretty lips,
Then put their nightgowns on.

As children caper when they wake,
Merry that it is morn,
My flowers from a hundred cribs
Will peep, and prance again.

6. Delight Becomes Pictorial

Delight becomes pictorial
When viewed through pain,
More fair, because impossible
That any gain.

The mountain at a given distance
In amber lies;
Approached, the amber flits a little,
And that's the skies!

7. Glee! The Great Storm Is Over!

Glee! The great storm is over!
Four have recovered the land;
Forty gone down together
Into the boiling sand.

Ring, for the scant salvation!
Toll, for the bonnie souls,
Neighbour and friend and bridegroom,
Spinning upon the shoals!

How they will tell the shipwreck
When winter shakes the door,
Till the children ask, "But the forty?
Did they come back no more?"

Then a silence suffuses the story,
And a softness the teller's eye;
And the children no further question,
And only the waves reply.

8. Have You Got A Brook In Your Little Heart

Have you got a brook in your little heart,
Where bashful flowers blow,
And blushing birds go down to drink,
And shadows tremble so?

And nobody knows, so still it flows,
That any brook is there;
And yet your little draught of life
Is daily drunken there.

Then look out for the little brook in March,
When the rivers overflow,
And the snows come hurrying from the hills,
And the bridges often go.

And later, in August it may be,
When the meadows parching lie,
Beware, lest this little brook of life
Some burning noon go dry!

9. I Asked No Other Thing

I asked no other thing,
No other was denied.
I offered Being for it;
The mighty merchant smiled.

Brazil? He twirled a button,
Without a glance my way:
"But, madam, is there nothing else
That we can show to-day?"

10. I Had No Time To Hate, Because

I had no time to hate, because
The grave would hinder me,
And life was not so ample I
Could finish enmity.

Nor had I time to love; but since
Some industry must be,
The little toil of love, I thought,
Was large enough for me.

11. I Have No Life but This

I have no life but this,
To lead it here;
Nor any death, but lest
Dispelled from there;

Nor tie to earths to come,
Nor action new,
Except through this extent,
The realm of you.

12. I Know A Place Where Summer Strives

I know a place where summer strives
With such a practised frost,
She each year leads her daisies back,
Recording briefly, "Lost."

But when the south wind stirs the pools
And struggles in the lanes,
Her heart misgives her for her vow,
And she pours soft refrains

Into the lap of adamant,
And spices, and the dew,
That stiffens quietly to quartz,
Upon her amber shoe.

13. I Taste A Liquor Never Brewed

I taste a liquor never brewed,
From tankards scooped in pearl;
Not all the vats upon the Rhine
Yield such an alcohol!

Inebriate of air am I,
And debauchee of dew,
Reeling, through endless summer days,
From inns of molten blue.

When landlords turn the drunken bee
Out of the foxglove's door,
When butterflies renounce their drams,
I shall but drink the more!

Till seraphs swing their snowy hats,
And saints to windows run,
To see the little tippler
Leaning against the sun!

14. If I Can Stop One Heart from Breaking

If I can stop one heart from breaking,
I shall not live in vain;
If I can ease one life the aching,
Or cool one pain,
Or help one fainting robin
Unto his nest again,
I shall not live in vain.

15. If I Should Die

If I should die,
And you should live,
And time should gurgle on,
And morn should beam,
And noon should burn,
As it has usual done;
If birds should build as early,
And bees as bustling go,
One might depart at option
From enterprise below!
'T is sweet to know that stocks will stand
When we with daisies lie,
That commerce will continue,
And trades as briskly fly.
It makes the parting tranquil
And keeps the soul serene,
That gentlemen so sprightly
Conduct the pleasing scene!

16. If You Were Coming In The Fall

If you were coming in the fall,
I'd brush the summer by
With half a smile and half a spurn,
As housewives do a fly.

If I could see you in a year,
I'd wind the months in balls,
And put them each in separate drawers,
Until their time befalls.

If only centuries delayed,
I'd count them on my hand,
Subtracting till my fingers dropped
Into Van Diemen's land.

If certain, when this life was out,
That yours and mine should be,
I'd toss it yonder like a rind,
And taste eternity.

But now, all ignorant of the length
Of time's uncertain wing,
It goads me, like the goblin bee,
That will not state its sting.

17. Is Heaven A Physician?

Is Heaven a physician?
They say that He can heal;
But medicine posthumous
Is unavailable.

Is Heaven an exchequer?
They speak of what we owe;
But that negotiation
I 'm not a party to.

18. Much Madness Is Divinest Sense

Much madness is divinest sense
To a discerning eye;
Much sense the starkest madness.
'T is the majority
In this, as all, prevails.
Assent, and you are sane;
Demur, you're straightway dangerous,
And handled with a chain.

19. New Feet Within My Garden Go

New feet within my garden go,
New fingers stir the sod;
A troubadour upon the elm
Betrays the solitude.

New children play upon the green,
New weary sleep below;
And still the pensive spring returns,
And still the punctual snow!

20. On This Long Storm The Rainbow Rose

On this long storm the rainbow rose,
On this late morn the sun;
The clouds, like listless elephants,
Horizons straggled down.

The birds rose smiling in their nests,
The gales indeed were done;
Alas! how heedless were the eyes
On whom the summer shone!

The quiet nonchalance of death
No daybreak can bestir;
The slow archangel's syllables
Must awaken her.

21. One Dignity Delays For All

One dignity delays for all,
One mitred afternoon.
None can avoid this purple,
None evade this crown.

Coach it insures, and footmen,
Chamber and state and throng;
Bells, also, in the village,
As we ride grand along.

What dignified attendants,
What service when we pause!
How loyally at parting
Their hundred hats they raise!

How pomp surpassing ermine,
When simple you and I
Present our meek escutcheon,
And claim the rank to die!

22. Belshazzar Had A Letter

Belshazzar had a letter,
He never had but one;
Belshazzar's correspondent
Concluded and begun
In that immortal copy
The conscience of us all
Can read without its glasses
On revelation's wall.

23. Our Share Of Night To Bear

Our share of night to bear,
Our share of morning,
Our blank in bliss to fill,
Our blank in scorning.

Here a star, and there a star,
Some lose their way.
Here a mist, and there a mist,
Afterwards   day!

24. Perhaps You'd Like To Buy A Flower?

Perhaps you'd like to buy a flower?
But I could never sell.
If you would like to borrow
Until the daffodil

Unties her yellow bonnet
Beneath the village door,
Until the bees, from clover rows
Their hock and sherry draw,

Why, I will lend until just then,
But not an hour more!

25. The Bee Is Not Afraid Of Me

The bee is not afraid of me,
I know the butterfly;
The pretty people in the woods
Receive me cordially.

The brooks laugh louder when I come,
The breezes madder play.
Wherefore, mine eyes, thy silver mists?
Wherefore, O summer's day?

26. The Brain Within Its Groove

The brain within its groove
Runs evenly and true;
But let a splinter swerve,
'T were easier for you
To put the water back
When floods have slit the hills,
And scooped a turnpike for themselves,
And blotted out the mills!

27. The Heart Asks Pleasure First

The heart asks pleasure first,
And then, excuse from pain;
And then, those little anodynes
That deaden suffering;

And then, to go to sleep;
And then, if it should be
The will of its Inquisitor,
The liberty to die.

28. The Pedigree of Honey

The pedigree of honey
Does not concern the bee;
A clover, any time, to him
Is aristocracy.

29. There's A Certain Slant Of Light

There's a certain slant of light,
On winter afternoons,
That oppresses, like the weight
Of cathedral tunes.

Heavenly hurt it gives us;
We can find no scar,
But internal difference
Where the meanings are.

None may teach it anything,
' T is the seal, despair,
An imperial affliction
Sent us of the air.

When it comes, the landscape listens,
Shadows hold their breath;
When it goes, 't is like the distance
On the look of death.

30. To Fight Aloud Is Very Brave

To fight aloud is very brave,
But gallanter, I know,
Who charge within the bosom,
The cavalry of woe.

Who win, and nations do not see,
Who fall, and none observe,
Whose dying eyes no country
Regards with patriot love.

We trust, in plumed procession,
For such the angels go,
Rank after rank, with even feet
And uniforms of snow.

31. Upon The Gallows Hung A Wretch

Upon the gallows hung a wretch,
Too sullied for the hell
To which the law entitled him.
As nature's curtain fell
The one who bore him tottered in,
For this was woman's son.
'"T was all I had,' she stricken gasped;
Oh, what a livid boon!

32. The One That Could Repeat the Summer Day

The one that could repeat the summer day
Were greater than itself, though he
Minutest of mankind might be.
And who could reproduce the sun,
At period of going down
The lingering and the stain, I mean
When Orient has been outgrown,
And Occident becomes unknown,
His name remain.

33. Whether My Bark Went Down At Sea

Whether my bark went down at sea,
Whether she met with gales,
Whether to isles enchanted
She bent her docile sails;

By what mystic mooring
She is held to-day,
This is the errand of the eye
Out upon the bay.

34. A Modest Lot, A Fame Petite

A modest lot, a fame petite,
A brief campaign of sting and sweet
Is plenty! Is enough!
A sailor's business is the shore,
A soldier's   balls. Who asketh more
Must seek the neighboring life!

35. A Well

What mystery pervades a well!
The water lives so far,
Like neighbor from another world
Residing in a jar.

The grass does not appear afraid;
I often wonder he
Can stand so close and look so bold
At what is dread to me.

Related somehow they may be,
The sedge stands next the sea,
Where he is floorless, yet of fear
No evidence gives he.

But nature is a stranger yet;
The ones that cite her most
Have never passed her haunted house,
Nor simplified her ghost.

To pity those that know her not
Is helped by the regret
That those who know her, know her less
The nearer her they get.

36. Who Robbed the Woods

Who robbed the woods,
The trusting woods?
The unsuspecting trees
Brought out their burrs and mosses
His fantasy to please.
He scanned their trinkets, curious,
He grasped, he bore away.
What will the solemn hemlock,
What will the fir-tree say?

37. Your Riches Taught Me Poverty

Your riches taught me poverty.
Myself a millionaire
In little wealth's,   as girls could boast,
Till broad as Buenos Ayre,

You drifted your dominions
A different Peru;
And I esteemed all poverty,
For life's estate with you.

Of mines I little know, myself,
But just the names of gems,
The colors of the commonest;
And scarce of diadems

So much that, did I meet the queen,
Her glory I should know:
But this must be a different wealth,
To miss it beggars so.

I 'm sure 't is India all day
To those who look on you
Without a stint, without a blame,
Might I but be the Jew!

I 'm sure it is Golconda,

Beyond my power to deem,
To have a smile for mine each day,
How better than a gem!
At least, it solaces to know
That there exists a gold,
Although I prove it just in time
Its distance to behold!

It 's far, far treasure to surmise,
And estimate the pearl
That slipped my simple fingers through
While just a girl at school!

38. A Book-I

He ate and drank the precious words,
His spirit grew robust;
He knew no more that he was poor,
Nor that his frame was dust.
He danced along the dingy days,
And this bequest of wings
Was but a book. What liberty
A loosened spirit brings!

39. A Book-II

There is no frigate like a book
To take us lands away,
Nor any coursers like a page
Of prancing poetry.
This traverse may the poorest take
Without oppress of toll;
How frugal is the chariot
That bears a human soul!

40. A Charm Invests A Face

A charm invests a face
Imperfectly beheld,
The lady dares not lift her veil
For fear it be dispelled.

But peers beyond her mesh,
And wishes, and denies,
Lest interview annul a want
That image satisfies.

41. A Clock Stopped Not The Mantel's

A Clock Stopped Not The Mantel's;
Geneva's farthest skill
Can't put the puppet bowing
That just now dangled still.

An awe came on the trinket!
The figures hunched with pain,
Then quivered out of decimals
Into degreeless noon.

It will not stir for doctors,
This pendulum of snow;
The shopman importunes it,
While cool, concern less No

Nods from the gilded pointers,
Nods from the seconds slim,
Decades of arrogance between
The dial life and him.

42. A Day

I'll tell you how the sun rose,
A ribbon at a time.
The steeples swam in amethyst,
The news like squirrels ran.

The hills untied their bonnets,
The bobolinks begun.
Then I said softly to myself,
"That must have been the sun!"

But how he set, I know not.
There seemed a purple stile
Which little yellow boys and girls
Were climbing all the while

Till when they reached the other side,
A dominie in Gray
Put gently up the evening bars,
And led the flock away.

43. A Death-Blow Is a Life-Blow to Some

A death-blow is a life-blow to some
Who, till they died, did not alive become;
Who, had they lived, had died, but when
They died, vitality begun.

44. A Dew Sufficed Itself

A dew sufficed itself
And satisfied a leaf,
And felt, 'how vast a destiny!
How trivial is life!'

The sun went out to work,
The day went out to play,
But not again that dew was seen
By physiognomy.

Whether by day abducted,
Or emptied by the sun
Into the sea, in passing,
Eternally unknown.

45. A Country Burial

Ample make this bed.
Make this bed with awe;
In it wait till judgment break
Excellent and fair.

Be its mattress straight,
Be its pillow round;
Let no sunrise' yellow noise
Interrupt this ground.

46. A Light Exists In Spring

A light exists in spring
Not present on the year
At any other period.
When March is scarcely here

A color stands abroad
On solitary hills
That science cannot overtake,
But human nature feels.

It waits upon the lawn;
It shows the furthest tree
Upon the furthest slope we know;
It almost speaks to me.

Then, as horizons step,
Or noons report away,
Without the formula of sound,
It passes, and we stay:

A quality of loss
Affecting our content,
As trade had suddenly encroached
Upon a sacrament.

47. A Murmur In The Trees To Note

A murmur in the trees to note,
Not loud enough for wind;
A star not far enough to seek,
Nor near enough to find;

A long, long yellow on the lawn,
A hubbub as of feet;
Not audible, as ours to us,
But dapperer, more sweet;

A hurrying home of little men
To houses unperceived,
All this, and more, if I should tell,
Would never be believed.

Of robins in the trundle bed
How many I espy
Whose nightgowns could not hide the wings,
Although I heard them try!

But then I promised ne'er to tell;
How could I break my word?
So go your way and I'll go mine,
No fear you'll miss the road.

48. A Poor Torn Heart, A Tattered Heart

A poor torn heart, a tattered heart,
That sat it down to rest,
Nor noticed that the ebbing day
Flowed silver to the west,
Nor noticed night did soft descend
Nor constellation burn,
Intent upon the vision
Of latitudes unknown.

The angels, happening that way,
This dusty heart espied;
Tenderly took it up from toil
And carried it to God.
There,   sandals for the barefoot;
There,   gathered from the gales,
Do the blue havens by the hand
Lead the wandering sails.

49. A Portrait.

A face devoid of love or grace,
A hateful, hard, successful face,
A face with which a stone
Would feel as thoroughly at ease
As were they old acquaintances,
First time together thrown.

50. A Prayer.

I meant to have but modest needs,
Such as content, and heaven;
Within my income these could lie,
And life and I keep even.

But since the last included both,
It would suffice my prayer
But just for one to stipulate,
And grace would grant the pair.

And so, upon this wise I prayed,
Great Spirit, give to me
A heaven not so large as yours,
But large enough for me.

A smile suffused Jehovah's face;
The cherubim withdrew;
Grave saints stole out to look at me,
And showed their dimples, too.

I left the place with all my might,
My prayer away I threw;
The quiet ages picked it up,
And Judgment twinkled, too,

That one so honest be extant
As take the tale for true
That "Whatsoever you shall ask,

Itself be given you."

But I, grown shrewder, scan the skies
With a suspicious air,
As children, swindled for the first,
All swindlers be, infer.

51. A Rose.

A sepal, petal, and a thorn
Upon a common summer's morn,
A flash of dew, a bee or two,
A breeze
A caper in the trees,
And I'm a rose!

52. A Snake.

Sweet is the swamp with its secrets,
Until we meet a snake;
'T is then we sigh for houses,
And our departure take
At that enthralling gallop
That only childhood knows.
A snake is summer's treason,
And guile is where it goes.

53. A Thunder-Storm

The wind begun to rock the grass
With threatening tunes and low,
He flung a menace at the earth,
A menace at the sky.

The leaves unhooked themselves from trees
And started all abroad;
The dust did scoop itself like hands
And throw away the road.

The wagons quickened on the streets,
The thunder hurried slow;
The lightning showed a yellow beak,
And then a livid claw.

The birds put up the bars to nests,
The cattle fled to barns;
There came one drop of giant rain,
And then, as if the hands

That held the dams had parted hold,
The waters wrecked the sky,
But overlooked my father's house,
Just quartering a tree.

54. A Word.

A word is dead
When it is said,
Some say.
I say it just
Begins to live
That day.

55. Adrift! A Little Boat Adrift!

Adrift! A little boat adrift!
And night is coming down!
Will no one guide a little boat
Unto the nearest town?

So, sailors say, on yesterday,
Just as the dusk was brown,
One little boat gave up its strife,
And gurgled down and down.

But angels say, on yesterday,
Just as the dawn was red,
One little boat overspent with gales
Retrimmed its masts, redecked its sails
Exultant, onward sped!

56. Afraid? Of Whom Am I Afraid?

Afraid? Of whom am I afraid?
Not death; for who is he?
The porter of my father's lodge
As much abashed me.

Of life? 'T were odd I fear a thing
That comprehended me
In one or more existences
At Deity's decree.

Of resurrection? Is the east
Afraid to trust the morn
With her fastidious forehead?
As soon impeach my crown!

57. April.

An altered look about the hills;
A Tyrian light the village fills;
A wider sunrise in the dawn;
A deeper twilight on the lawn;
A print of a vermilion foot;
A purple finger on the slope;
A flippant fly upon the pane;
A spider at his trade again;
An added strut in chanticleer;
A flower expected everywhere;
An axe shrill singing in the woods;
Fern-odors on untravelled roads,
All this, and more I cannot tell,
A furtive look you know as well,
And Nicodemus' mystery
Receives its annual reply.

58. Alpine Glow.

Our lives are Swiss,
So still, so cool,
Till, some odd afternoon,
The Alps neglect their curtains,
And we look farther on.

Italy stands the other side,
While, like a guard between,
The solemn Alps,
The siren Alps,
Forever intervene!

59. High From The Earth I Heard A Bird

High from the earth I heard a bird;
He trod upon the trees
As he esteemed them trifles,
And then he spied a breeze,
And situated softly
Upon a pile of wind
Which in a perturbation
Nature had left behind.
A joyous-going fellow
I gathered from his talk,
Which both of benediction
And badinage partook,
Without apparent burden,
I learned, in leafy wood
He was the faithful father
Of a dependent brood;
And this untoward transport
His remedy for care,
A contrast to our respites.
How different we are!

60. As By The Dead We Love To Sit

As by the dead we love to sit,
Become so wondrous dear,
As for the lost we grapple,
Though all the rest are here,

In broken mathematics
We estimate our prize,
Vast, in its fading ratio,
Aspiration.

We never know how high we are
Till we are called to rise;
And then, if we are true to plan,
Our statures touch the skies.

The heroism we recite
Would be a daily thing,
Did not ourselves the cubits warp
For fear to be a king.

61. Asleep

As far from pity as complaint,
As cool to speech as stone,
As numb to revelation
As if my trade were bone.

As far from time as history,
As near yourself to-day
As children to the rainbow's scarf,
Or sunset's yellow play

To eyelids in the sepulchre.
How still the dancer lies,
While color's revelations break,
And blaze the butterflies!

62. Apotheosis.

Come slowly, Eden!
Lips unused to thee,
Bashful, sip thy jasmines,
As the fainting bee,

Reaching late his flower,
Round her chamber hums,
Counts his nectars   enters,
And is lost in balms!

63. Apocalypse.

I'm wife; I've finished that,
That other state;
I'm Czar, I'm woman now:
It's safer so.

How odd the girl's life looks
Behind this soft eclipse!
I think that earth seems so
To those in heaven now.

This being comfort, then
That other kind was pain;
But why compare?
I'm wife! stop there!

64. Aftermath.

The murmuring of bees has ceased;
But murmuring of some
Posterior, prophetic,
Has simultaneous come,

The lower metres of the year,
When nature's laugh is done,
The Revelations of the book
Whose Genesis is June.

65. A Toad Can Die Of Light!

A toad can die of light!
Death is the common right
Of toads and men,
Of earl and midge
The privilege.
Why swagger then?
The gnat's supremacy
Is large as thine.

66. A Sickness Of This World It Most Occasions

A sickness of this world it most occasions
When best men die;
A wishfulness their far condition
To occupy.

A chief indifference, as foreign
A world must be
Themselves forsake contented,
For Deity.

67. A Service Of Song.

Some keep the Sabbath going to church;
I keep it staying at home,
With a bobolink for a chorister,
And an orchard for a dome.

Some keep the Sabbath in surplice;
I just wear my wings,
And instead of tolling the bell for church,
Our little sexton sings.

God preaches,   a noted clergyman,
And the sermon is never long;
So instead of getting to heaven at last,
I'm going all along!

68. A Man.

Fate slew him, but he did not drop;
She felled   he did not fall
Impaled him on her fiercest stakes
He neutralized them all.

She stung him, sapped his firm advance,
But, when her worst was done,
And he, unmoved, regarded her,
Acknowledged him a man.

69. At Least To Pray Is Left, Is Left.

At least to pray is left, is left.
O Jesus! in the air
I know not which thy chamber is,
I 'm knocking everywhere.

Thou stirrest earthquake in the South,
And maelstrom in the sea;
Say, Jesus Christ of Nazareth,
Hast thou no arm for me?

70. Could I But Ride Indefinite

Could I but ride indefinite,
As doth the meadow-bee,
And visit only where I liked,
And no man visit me,

And flirt all day with buttercups,
And marry whom I may,
And dwell a little everywhere,
Or better, run away

With no police to follow,
Or chase me if I do,
Till I should jump peninsulas
To get away from you,

I said, but just to be a bee
Upon a raft of air,
And row in nowhere all day long,
And anchor off the bar,
What liberty! So captives deem
Who tight in dungeons are.

71. Aurora.

Of bronze and blaze
The north, to-night!
So adequate its forms,
So preconcerted with itself,
So distant to alarms,
An unconcern so sovereign
To universe, or me,
It paints my simple spirit
With tints of majesty,
Till I take vaster attitudes,
And strut upon my stem,
Disdaining men and oxygen,
For arrogance of them.

My splendours are menagerie;
But their compete less show
Will entertain the centuries
When I am, long ago,
An island in dishonoured grass,
Whom none but daisies know.

72. Autumn.

The morns are meeker than they were,
The nuts are getting brown;
The berry's cheek is plumper,
The rose is out of town.

The maple wears a gayer scarf,
The field a scarlet gown.
Lest I should be old-fashioned,
I'll put a trinket on.

73. By The Sea.

I started early, took my dog,
And visited the sea;
The mermaids in the basement
Came out to look at me,

And frigates in the upper floor
Extended hempen hands,
Presuming me to be a mouse
Aground, upon the sands.

But no man moved me till the tide
Went past my simple shoe,
And past my apron and my belt,
And past my bodice too,

And made as he would eat me up
As wholly as a dew
Upon a dandelion's sleeve
And then I started too.

And he   he followed close behind;
I felt his silver heel
Upon my ankle,   then my shoes
Would overflow with pearl.

Until we met the solid town,
No man he seemed to know;
And bowing with a mighty look

At me, the sea withdrew.

74. Childish Griefs.

Softened by Time's consummate plush,
How sleek the woe appears
That threatened childhood's citadel
And undermined the years!

Bisected now by bleaker griefs,
We envy the despair
That devastated childhood's realm,
So easy to repair.

75. Before The Ice Is In The Pools

Before the ice is in the pools,
Before the skaters go,
Or any cheek at nightfall
Is tarnished by the snow,

Before the fields have finished,
Before the Christmas tree,
Wonder upon wonder
Will arrive to me!

What we touch the hems of
On a summer's day;
What is only walking
Just a bridge away;

That which sings so, speaks so,
When there's no one here,
Will the frock I wept in
Answer me to wear?

76. Beclouded.

The sky is low, the clouds are mean,
A travelling flake of snow
Across a barn or through a rut
Debates if it will go.

A narrow wind complains all day
How someone treated him;
Nature, like us, is sometimes caught
Without her diadem.

77. At Home.

The night was wide, and furnished scant
With but a single star,
That often as a cloud it met
Blew out itself for fear.

The wind pursued the little bush,
And drove away the leaves
November left; then clambered up
And fretted in the eaves.

No squirrel went abroad;
A dog's belated feet
Like intermittent plush were heard
Adown the empty street.

To feel if blinds be fast,
And closer to the fire
Her little rocking-chair to draw,
And shiver for the poor,

The housewife's gentle task.
"How pleasanter," said she
Unto the sofa opposite,
"The sleet than May   no thee!"

78. Astra Castra.

Departed to the judgment,
A mighty afternoon;
Great clouds like ushers leaning,
Creation looking on.

The flesh surrendered, cancelled,
The bodiless begun;
Two worlds, like audiences, disperse
And leave the soul alone.

79. Cobwebs.

The spider as an artist
Has never been employed
Though his surpassing merit
Is freely certified

By every broom and Bridget
Throughout a Christian land.
Neglected son of genius,
I take thee by the hand.

80. Dawn-I

When night is almost done,
And sunrise grows so near
That we can touch the spaces,
It's time to smooth the hair

And get the dimples ready,
And wonder we could care
For that old faded midnight
That frightened but an hour.

81. Dawn-II

Not knowing when the dawn will come
I open every door;
Or has it feathers like a bird,
Or billows like a shore?

82. Cocoon.

Drab habitation of whom?
Tabernacle or tomb,
Or dome of worm,
Or porch of gnome,
Or some elf's catacomb?

83. Choice.

Of all the souls that stand create
I have elected one.
When sense from spirit files away,
And subterfuge is done;

When that which is and that which was
Apart, intrinsic, stand,
And this brief tragedy of flesh
Is shifted like a sand;

When figures show their royal front
And mists are carved away,
Behold the atom I preferred
To all the lists of clay!

84. Contrast.

A door just opened on a street
I, lost, was passing by
An instant's width of warmth disclosed,
And wealth, and company.

The door as sudden shut, and I,
I, lost, was passing by,
Lost doubly, but by contrast most,
Enlightening misery.

85. Consecration.

Proud of my broken heart since thou didst break it,
Proud of the pain I did not feel till thee,
Proud of my night since thou with moons dost slake it,
Not to partake thy passion, my humility.

86. Dead.

There's something quieter than sleep
Within this inner room!
It wears a sprig upon its breast,
And will not tell its name.

Some touch it and some kiss it,
Some chafe its idle hand;
It has a simple gravity
I do not understand!

While simple-hearted neighbors
Chat of the 'early dead,'
We, prone to periphrasis,
Remark that birds have fled!

87. Death And Life

Apparently with no surprise
To any happy flower,
The frost beheads it at its play
In accidental power.
The blond assassin passes on,
The sun proceeds unmoved
To measure off another day
For an approving God.

88. Death Is A Dialogue Between

Death is a dialogue between
The spirit and the dust.
"Dissolve," says Death. The Spirit, "Sir,
I have another trust."

Death doubts it, argues from the ground.
The Spirit turns away,
Just laying off, for evidence,
An overcoat of clay.

89. Death.

Death is like the insect
Menacing the tree,
Competent to kill it,
But decoyed may be.

Bait it with the balsam,
Seek it with the knife,
Baffle, if it cost you
Everything in life.

Then, if it have burrowed
Out of reach of skill,
Ring the tree and leave it,
'T is the vermin's will.

90. Dreams.

Let me not mar that perfect dream
By an auroral stain,
But so adjust my daily night
That it will come again.

91. Each That We Lose Takes Part Of Us.

Each that we lose takes part of us;
A crescent still abides,
Which like the moon, some turbid night,
Is summoned by the tides.

92. Eternity.

On this wondrous sea,
Sailing silently,
Ho! pilot, ho!
Knowest thou the shore
Where no breakers roar,
Where the storm is o'er?

In the silent west
Many sails at rest,
Their anchors fast;
Thither I pilot thee,
Land, ho! Eternity!
Ashore at last!

93. Evening.

The cricket sang,
And set the sun,
And workmen finished, one by one,
Their seam the day upon.

The low grass loaded with the dew,
The twilight stood as strangers do
With hat in hand, polite and new,
To stay as if, or go.

A vastness, as a neighbor, came,
A wisdom without face or name,
A peace, as hemispheres at home,
And so the night became.

94. Exclusion.

The soul selects her own society,
Then shuts the door;
On her divine majority
Obtrude no more.

Unmoved, she notes the chariot's pausing
At her low gate;
Unmoved, an emperor is kneeling
Upon her mat.

I've known her from an ample nation
Choose one;
Then close the valves of her attention
Like stone.

95. Fire.

Ashes denote that fire was;
Respect the grayest pile
For the departed creature's sake
That hovered there awhile.

Fire exists the first in light,
And then consolidates,
Only the chemist can disclose
Into what carbonates.

96. Friends.

Are friends delight or pain?
Could bounty but remain
Riches were good.

But if they only stay
Bolder to fly away,
Riches are sad.

97. Ghosts.

One need not be a chamber to be haunted,
One need not be a house;
The brain has corridors surpassing
Material place.

Far safer, of a midnight meeting
External ghost,
Than an interior confronting
That whiter host.

Far safer through an Abbey gallop,
The stones achase,
Than, moonless, one's own self encounter
In lonesome place.

Ourself, behind ourself concealed,
Should startle most;
Assassin, hid in our apartment,
Be horror's least.

The prudent carries a revolver,
He bolts the door,
O'erlooking a superior spectre
More near.

98. Hope-I

Hope is the thing with feathers
That perches in the soul,
And sings the tune without the words,
And never stops at all,

And sweetest in the gale is heard;
And sore must be the storm
That could abash the little bird
That kept so many warm.

I 've heard it in the chillest land,
And on the strangest sea;
Yet, never, in extremity,
It asked a crumb of me.

99. Hope–II

Hope is a subtle glutton;
He feeds upon the fair;
And yet, inspected closely,
What abstinence is there!

His is the halcyon table
That never seats but one,
And whatsoever is consumed
The same amounts remain.

100. I Bring An Unaccustomed Wine

I bring an unaccustomed wine
To lips long parching, next to mine,
And summon them to drink.

Crackling with fever, they essay;
I turn my brimming eyes away,
And come next hour to look.

The hands still hug the tardy glass;
The lips I would have cooled, alas!
Are so superfluous cold,

I would as soon attempt to warm
The bosoms where the frost has lain
Ages beneath the mould.

Some other thirsty there may be
To whom this would have pointed me
Had it remained to speak.

And so I always bear the cup
If, haply, mine may be the drop
Some pilgrim thirst to slake,

If, haply, any say to me,
"Unto the little, unto me,"

When I at last awake.

101. I Felt A Funeral In My Brain

I felt a funeral in my brain,
And mourners, to and fro,
Kept treading, treading, till it seemed
That sense was breaking through.

And when they all were seated,
A service like a drum
Kept beating, beating, till I thought
My mind was going numb.

And then I heard them lift a box,
And creak across my soul
With those same boots of lead, again.
Then space began to toll

As all the heavens were a bell,
And Being but an ear,
And I and silence some strange race,
Wrecked, solitary, here.

102. I Never Saw A Moor

I never saw a moor,
I never saw the sea;
Yet know I how the heather looks,
And what a wave must be.

I never spoke with God,
Nor visited in heaven;
Yet certain am I of the spot
As if the chart were given.

103. I'm Nobody!

I'm Nobody!Who are you?
Are you nobody, too?
Then there's a pair of us   don't tell!
They 'd banish us, you know.

How dreary to be somebody!
How public, like a frog
To tell your name the livelong day
To an admiring bog!

104. Dying-I

The sun kept setting, setting still;
No hue of afternoon
Upon the village I perceived,
From house to house 't was noon.

The dusk kept dropping, dropping still;
No dew upon the grass,
But only on my forehead stopped,
And wandered in my face.

My feet kept drowsing, drowsing still,
My fingers were awake;
Yet why so little sound myself
Unto my seeming make?

How well I knew the light before!
I could not see it now.
'T is dying, I am doing; but
I'm not afraid to know.

105. Dying-II

I heard a fly buzz when I died;
The stillness round my form
Was like the stillness in the air
Between the heaves of storm.

The eyes beside had wrung them dry,
And breaths were gathering sure
For that last onset, when the king
Be witnessed in his power.

I willed my keepsakes, signed away
What portion of me I
Could make assignable,   and then
There interposed a fly,

With blue, uncertain, stumbling buzz,
Between the light and me;
And then the windows failed, and then
I could not see to see.

106. Desire.

Who never wanted,   maddest joy
Remains to him unknown:
The banquet of abstemiousness
Surpasses that of wine.

Within its hope, though yet ungrasped
Desire's perfect goal,
No nearer, lest reality
Should disenthrall thy soul.

107. Emancipation.

No rack can torture me,
My soul's at liberty
Behind this mortal bone
There knits a bolder one

You cannot prick with saw,
Nor rend with scymitar.
Two bodies therefore be;
Bind one, and one will flee.

The eagle of his nest
No easier divest
And gain the sky,
Than mayest thou,

Except thyself may be
Thine enemy;
Captivity is consciousness,
So's liberty.

108. Enough.

God gave a loaf to every bird,
But just a crumb to me;
I dare not eat it, though I starve,
My poignant luxury
To own it, touch it, prove the feat
That made the pellet mine,
Too happy in my sparrow chance
For ampler coveting.

It might be famine all around,
I could not miss an ear,
Such plenty smiles upon my board,
My garner shows so fair.
I wonder how the rich may feel,
An Indiaman   an Earl?
I deem that I with but a crumb
Am sovereign of them all.

109. Ending.

That is solemn we have ended,
Be it but a play,
Or a glee among the garrets,
Or a holiday,

Or a leaving home; or later,
Parting with a world
We have understood, for better
Still it be unfurled.

110. Far From Love The Heavenly Father

Far from love the Heavenly Father
Leads the chosen child;
Oftener through realm of briar
Than the meadow mild,

Oftener by the claw of dragon
Than the hand of friend,
Guides the little one predestined
To the native land.

111. Few Get Enough

Few get enough,   enough is one;
To that ethereal throng
Have not each one of us the right
To stealthily belong?

112. Griefs

I measure every grief I meet
With analytic eyes;
I wonder if it weighs like mine,
Or has an easier size.

I wonder if they bore it long,
Or did it just begin?
I could not tell the date of mine,
It feels so old a pain.

I wonder if it hurts to live,
And if they have to try,
And whether, could they choose between,
They would not rather die.

I wonder if when years have piled
Some thousands   on the cause
Of early hurt, if such a lapse
Could give them any pause;

Or would they go on aching still
Through centuries above,
Enlightened to a larger pain
By contrast with the love.

The grieved are many, I am told;
The reason deeper lies,
Death is but one and comes but once,

And only nails the eyes.

There's grief of want, and grief of cold,
A sort they call 'despair;'
There's banishment from native eyes,
In sight of native air.

And though I may not guess the kind
Correctly, yet to me
A piercing comfort it affords
In passing Calvary,

To note the fashions of the cross,
Of those that stand alone,
Still fascinated to presume
That some are like my own.

113. Going.

On such a night, or such a night,
Would anybody care
If such a little figure
Slipped quiet from its chair,

So quiet, oh, how quiet!
That nobody might know
But that the little figure
Rocked softer, to and fro?

On such a dawn, or such a dawn,
Would anybody sigh
That such a little figure
Too sound asleep did lie

For chanticleer to wake it,
Or stirring house below,
Or giddy bird in orchard,
Or early task to do?

There was a little figure plump
For every little knoll,
Busy needles, and spools of thread,
And trudging feet from school.

Playmates, and holidays, and nuts,
And visions vast and small.
Strange that the feet so precious charged

Should reach so small a goal!

114. Going To Heaven!

Going to heaven!
I don't know when,
Pray do not ask me how,
Indeed, I 'm too astonished
To think of answering you!
Going to heaven!
How dim it sounds!
And yet it will be done
As sure as flocks go home at night
Unto the shepherd's arm!

Perhaps you 're going too!
Who knows?
If you should get there first,
Save just a little place for me
Close to the two I lost!

The smallest "robe" will fit me,
And just a bit of "crown;"
For you know we do not mind our dress
When we are going home.

I 'm glad I don't believe it,
For it would stop my breath,
And I 'd like to look a little more
At such a curious earth!
I am glad they did believe it

Whom I have never found
Since the mighty autumn afternoon
I left them in the ground.

115. Forbidden Fruit-I

Forbidden fruit a flavor has
That lawful orchards mocks;
How luscious lies the pea within
The pod that Duty locks!

116. Forbidden Fruit-II

Heaven is what I cannot reach!
The apple on the tree,
Provided it do hopeless hang,
That 'heaven' is, to me.

The color on the cruising cloud,
The interdicted ground
Behind the hill, the house behind,
There Paradise is found!

117. Father, I Bring Thee Not Myself

Father, I bring thee not myself,
That were the little load;
I bring thee the imperial heart
I had not strength to hold.

The heart I cherished in my own
Till mine too heavy grew,
Yet strangest, heavier since it went,
Is it too large for you?

118. Farewell

Tie the strings to my life, my Lord,
Then I am ready to go!
Just a look at the horses
Rapid! That will do!

Put me in on the firmest side,
So I shall never fall;
For we must ride to the Judgment,
And it's partly down hill.

But never I mind the bridges,
And never I mind the sea;
Held fast in everlasting race
By my own choice and thee.

Good-by to the life I used to live,
And the world I used to know;
And kiss the hills for me, just once;
Now I am ready to go!

119. Faith Is A Fine Invention

Faith is a fine invention
For gentlemen who see;
But microscopes are prudent
In an emergency!

120. Escape.

I never hear the word "escape"
Without a quicker blood,
A sudden expectation,
A flying attitude.

I never hear of prisons broad
By soldiers battered down,
But I tug childish at my bars,
Only to fail again!

121. In The Garden.

A bird came down the walk:
He did not know I saw;
He bit an angle-worm in halves
And ate the fellow, raw.

And then he drank a dew
From a convenient grass,
And then hopped sidewise to the wall
To let a beetle pass.

He glanced with rapid eyes
That hurried all abroad,
They looked like frightened beads, I thought;
He stirred his velvet head

Like one in danger; cautious,
I offered him a crumb,
And he unrolled his feathers
And rowed him softer home

Than oars divide the ocean,
Too silver for a seam,
Or butterflies, off banks of noon,
Leap, plashless, as they swim.

122. Lost.

I lost a world the other day.
Has anybody found?
You'll know it by the row of stars
Around its forehead bound.

A rich man might not notice it;
Yet to my frugal eye
Of more esteem than ducats.
Oh, find it, sir, for me!

123. Love.

Love is anterior to life,
Posterior to death,
Initial of creation, and
The exponent of breath.

124. Lost Faith

To lose one's faith surpasses
The loss of an estate,
Because estates can be
Replenished,   faith cannot.

Inherited with life,
Belief but once can be;
Annihilate a single clause,
And Being's beggary.

125. Look Back On Time With Kindly Eyes

Look back on time with kindly eyes,
He doubtless did his best;
How softly sinks his trembling sun
In human nature's west!

126. Longing.

I envy seas whereon he rides,
I envy spokes of wheels
Of chariots that him convey,
I envy speechless hills

That gaze upon his journey;
How easy all can see
What is forbidden utterly
As heaven, unto me!

I envy nests of sparrows
That dot his distant eaves,
The wealthy fly upon his pane,
The happy, happy leaves

That just abroad his window
Have summer's leave to be,
The earrings of Pizarro
Could not obtain for me.

I envy light that wakes him,
And bells that boldly ring
To tell him it is noon abroad,
Myself his noon could bring,

Yet interdict my blossom
And abrogate my bee,
Lest noon in everlasting night

Drop Gabriel and me.

127. It Was Not Death, For I Stood Up

It was not death, for I stood up,
And all the dead lie down;
It was not night, for all the bells
Put out their tongues, for noon.

It was not frost, for on my flesh
I felt siroccos crawl,
Nor fire, for just my marble feet
Could keep a chancel cool.

And yet it tasted like them all;
The figures I have seen
Set orderly, for burial,
Reminded me of mine,

As if my life were shaven
And fitted to a frame,
And could not breathe without a key;
And 't was like midnight, some,

When everything that ticked has stopped,
And space stares, all around,
Or grisly frosts, first autumn morns,
Repeal the beating ground.

But most like chaos,   stopless, cool,
Without a chance or spar,
Or even a report of land
To justify despair.

128. Invisible.

From us she wandered now a year,
Her tarrying unknown;
If wilderness prevent her feet,
Or that ethereal zone

No eye hath seen and lived,
We ignorant must be.
We only know what time of year
We took the mystery.

129. In A Library

A precious, mouldering pleasure 't is
To meet an antique book,
In just the dress his century wore;
A privilege, I think,

His venerable hand to take,
And warming in our own,
A passage back, or two, to make
To times when he was young.

His quaint opinions to inspect,
His knowledge to unfold
On what concerns our mutual mind,
The literature of old;

What interested scholars most,
What competitions ran
When Plato was a certainty.
And Sophocles a man;

When Sappho was a living girl,
And Beatrice wore
The gown that Dante deified.
Facts, centuries before,

He traverses familiar,
As one should come to town
And tell you all your dreams were true;

He lived where dreams were sown.

His presence is enchantment,
You beg him not to go;
Old volumes shake their vellum heads
And tantalize, just so.

130. Immortality.

It is an honorable thought,
And makes one lift one's hat,
As one encountered gentlefolk
Upon a daily street,

That we've immortal place,
Though pyramids decay,
And kingdoms, like the orchard,
Flit russetly away.

131. I Wish I Knew That Woman's Name

I wish I knew that woman's name,
So, when she comes this way,
To hold my life, and hold my ears,
For fear I hear her say

She's 'sorry I am dead,' again,
Just when the grave and I
Have sobbed ourselves almost to sleep,
Our only lullaby.

132. I Know That He Exists

I know that he exists
Somewhere, in silence.
He has hid his rare life
From our gross eyes.

'T is an instant's play,
'T is a fond ambush,
Just to make bliss
Earn her own surprise!

But should the play
Prove piercing earnest,
Should the glee glaze
In death's stiff stare,

Would not the fun
Look too expensive?
Would not the jest
Have crawled too far?

133. I Have Not Told My Garden Yet

I have not told my garden yet,
Lest that should conquer me;
I have not quite the strength now
To break it to the bee.

I will not name it in the street,
For shops would stare, that I,
So shy, so very ignorant,
Should have the face to die.

The hillsides must not know it,
Where I have rambled so,
Nor tell the loving forests
The day that I shall go,

Nor lisp it at the table,
Nor heedless by the way
Hint that within the riddle
One will walk to-day!

134. He Touched Me, So I Live To Know

He touched me, so I live to know
That such a day, permitted so,
I groped upon his breast.
It was a boundless place to me,
And silenced, as the awful sea
Puts minor streams to rest.

And now, I'm different from before,
As if I breathed superior air,
Or brushed a royal gown;
My feet, too, that had wandered so,
My gypsy face transfigured now
To tenderer renown.

135. Mother Nature

Nature, the gentlest mother,
Impatient of no child,
The feeblest or the waywardest,
Her admonition mild

In forest and the hill
By traveller is heard,
Restraining rampant squirrel
Or too impetuous bird.

How fair her conversation,
A summer afternoon,
Her household, her assembly;
And when the sun goes down

Her voice among the aisles
Incites the timid prayer
Of the minutest cricket,
The most unworthy flower.

When all the children sleep
She turns as long away
As will suffice to light her lamps;
Then, bending from the sky

With infinite affection
And infiniter care,
Her golden finger on her lip,

Wills silence everywhere.

136. Nature Rarer Uses Yellow

Nature rarer uses yellow
Than another hue;
Saves she all of that for sunsets,
Prodigal of blue,

Spending scarlet like a woman,
Yellow she affords
Only scantly and selectly,
Like a lover's words.

137. Real.

I like a look of agony,
Because I know it's true;
Men do not sham convulsion,
Nor simulate a throe.

The eyes glaze once, and that is death.
Impossible to feign
The beads upon the forehead
By homely anguish strung.

138. Summer Shower.

A drop fell on the apple tree,
Another on the roof;
A half a dozen kissed the eaves,
And made the gables laugh.

A few went out to help the brook,
That went to help the sea.
Myself conjectured, Were they pearls,
What necklaces could be!

The dust replaced in hoisted roads,
The birds jocoser sung;
The sunshine threw his hat away,
The orchards spangles hung.

The breezes brought dejected lutes,
And bathed them in the glee;
The East put out a single flag,
And signed the fete away.

139. Sunset-I

Where ships of purple gently toss
On seas of daffodil,
Fantastic sailors mingle,
And then   the wharf is still.

140. Sunset-II

A sloop of amber slips away
Upon an ether sea,
And wrecks in peace a purple tar,
The son of ecstasy.
Purple Clover.

There is a flower that bees prefer,
And butterflies desire;
To gain the purple democrat
The humming-birds aspire.

And whatsoever insect pass,
A honey bears away
Proportioned to his several dearth
And her capacity.

Her face is rounder than the moon,
And ruddier than the gown
Of orchis in the pasture,
Or rhododendron worn.

She doth not wait for June;
Before the world is green
Her sturdy little countenance
Against the wind is seen,

Contending with the grass,
Near kinsman to herself,

For privilege of sod and sun,
Sweet litigants for life.
And when the hills are full,
And newer fashions blow,
Doth not retract a single spice
For pang of jealousy.

Her public is the noon,
Her providence the sun,
Her progress by the bee proclaimed
In sovereign, swerveless tune.

The bravest of the host,
Surrendering the last,
Nor even of defeat aware
When cancelled by the frost.

141. Power.

You cannot put a fire out;
A thing that can ignite
Can go, itself, without a fan
Upon the slowest night.

You cannot fold a flood
And put it in a drawer,
Because the winds would find it out,
And tell your cedar floor.

142. Out Of The Morning

Will there really be a morning?
Is there such a thing as day?
Could I see it from the mountains
If I were as tall as they?

Has it feet like water-lilies?
Has it feathers like a bird?
Is it brought from famous countries
Of which I have never heard?

Oh, some scholar! Oh, some sailor!
Oh, some wise man from the skies!
Please to tell a little pilgrim
Where the place called morning lies!

143. November.

Besides the autumn poets sing,
A few prosaic days
A little this side of the snow
And that side of the haze.

A few incisive mornings,
A few ascetic eyes,
Gone Mr. Bryant's golden-rod,
And Mr. Thomson's sheaves.

Still is the bustle in the brook,
Sealed are the spicy valves;
Mesmeric fingers softly touch
The eyes of many elves.

Perhaps a squirrel may remain,
My sentiments to share.
Grant me, O Lord, a sunny mind,
Thy windy will to bear!

144. Morning Is The Place For Dew

Morning is the place for dew,
Corn is made at noon,
After dinner light for flowers,
Dukes for setting sun!

145. Melodies Unheard

Musicians wrestle everywhere:
All day, among the crowded air,
I hear the silver strife;
And waking long before the dawn
Such transport breaks upon the town
I think it that "new life!"

It is not bird, it has no nest;
Nor band, in brass and scarlet dressed,
Nor tambourine, nor man;
It is not hymn from pulpit read,
The morning stars the treble led
On time's first afternoon!

Some say it is the spheres at play!
Some say that bright majority
Of vanished dames and men!
Some think it service in the place
Where we, with late, celestial face,
Please God, shall ascertain!

146. May-Flower

Pink, small, and punctual,
Aromatic, low,
Covert in April,
Candid in May,

Dear to the moss,
Known by the knoll,
Next to the robin
In every human soul.

Bold little beauty,
Bedecked with thee,
Nature forswears
Antiquity.

147. The Bee

Like trains of cars on tracks of plush
I hear the level bee:
A jar across the flowers goes,
Their velvet masonry

Withstands until the sweet assault
Their chivalry consumes,
While he, victorious, tilts away
To vanquish other blooms.

His feet are shod with gauze,
His helmet is of gold;
His breast, a single onyx
With chrysoprase, inlaid.

His labor is a chant,
His idleness a tune;
Oh, for a bee's experience
Of clovers and of noon!

148. The Chariot

Because I could not stop for Death,
He kindly stopped for me;
The carriage held but just ourselves
And Immortality.

We slowly drove, he knew no haste,
And I had put away
My labor, and my leisure too,
For his civility.

We passed the school where children played,
Their lessons scarcely done;
We passed the fields of gazing grain,
We passed the setting sun.

We paused before a house that seemed
A swelling of the ground;
The roof was scarcely visible,
The cornice but a mound.

Since then 't is centuries; but each
Feels shorter than the day
I first surmised the horses' heads
Were toward eternity.

149. The Grass

The grass so little has to do,
A sphere of simple green,
With only butterflies to brood,
And bees to entertain,

And stir all day to pretty tunes
The breezes fetch along,
And hold the sunshine in its lap
And bow to everything;

And thread the dews all night, like pearls,
And make itself so fine,
A duchess were too common
For such a noticing.

And even when it dies, to pass
In odors so divine,
As lowly spices gone to sleep,
Or amulets of pine.

And then to dwell in sovereign barns,
And dream the days away,
The grass so little has to do,
I wish I were the hay!

150. The Moon Is Distant From The Sea

The moon is distant from the sea,
And yet with amber hands
She leads him, docile as a boy,
Along appointed sands.

He never misses a degree;
Obedient to her eye,
He comes just so far toward the town,
Just so far goes away.

Oh, Signor, thine the amber hand,
And mine the distant sea,
Obedient to the least command
Thine eyes impose on me.

151. The Moon

The moon was but a chin of gold
A night or two ago,
And now she turns her perfect face
Upon the world below.

Her forehead is of amplest blond;
Her cheek like beryl stone;
Her eye unto the summer dew
The likest I have known.

Her lips of amber never part;
But what must be the smile
Upon her friend she could bestow
Were such her silver will!

And what a privilege to be
But the remotest star!
For certainly her way might pass
Beside your twinkling door.

Her bonnet is the firmament,
The universe her shoe,
The stars the trinkets at her belt,
Her dimities of blue.

152. The Sea

An everywhere of silver,
With ropes of sand
To keep it from effacing
The track called land.

153. The Tulip

She slept beneath a tree
Remembered but by me.
I touched her cradle mute;
She recognized the foot,
Put on her carmine suit,
And see!

154. Waiting.

I sing to use the waiting,
My bonnet but to tie,
And shut the door unto my house;
No more to do have I,

Till, his best step approaching,
We journey to the day,
And tell each other how we sang
To keep the dark away.

155. The Daisy Follows Soft The Sun

The daisy follows soft the sun,
And when his golden walk is done,
Sits shyly at his feet.
He, waking, finds the flower near.
"Wherefore, marauder, art thou here?"
"Because, sir, love is sweet!"

We are the flower, Thou the sun!
Forgive us, if as days decline,
We nearer steal to Thee,
Enamoured of the parting west,
The peace, the flight, the amethyst,
Night's possibility!

156. The Bluebird

Before you thought of spring,
Except as a surmise,
You see, God bless his suddenness,
A fellow in the skies
Of independent hues,
A little weather-worn,
Inspiriting habiliments
Of indigo and brown.

With specimens of song,
As if for you to choose,
Discretion in the interval,
With gay delays he goes
To some superior tree
Without a single leaf,
And shouts for joy to nobody
But his seraphic self!

157. The Bat

The bat is dun with wrinkled wings
Like fallow article,
And not a song pervades his lips,
Or none perceptible.

His small umbrella, quaintly halved,
Describing in the air
An arc alike inscrutable,
Elate philosopher!

Deputed from what firmament
Of what astute abode,
Empowered with what malevolence
Auspiciously withheld.

To his adroit Creator
Ascribe no less the praise;
Beneficent, believe me,
His eccentricities.

158. Success.

Success is counted sweetest
By those who ne'er succeed.
To comprehend a nectar
Requires sorest need.

Not one of all the purple host
Who took the flag to-day
Can tell the definition,
So clear, of victory,

As he, defeated, dying,
On whose forbidden ear
The distant strains of triumph
Break, agonized and clear!

159. Storm.

It sounded as if the streets were running,
And then the streets stood still.
Eclipse was all we could see at the window,
And awe was all we could feel.

By and by the boldest stole out of his covert,
To see if time was there.
Nature was in her beryl apron,
Mixing fresher air.

160. Some, Too Fragile For Winter Winds

Some, too fragile for winter winds,
The thoughtful grave encloses,
Tenderly tucking them in from frost
Before their feet are cold.

Never the treasures in her nest
The cautious grave exposes,
Building where schoolboy dare not look
And sportsman is not bold.

This covert have all the children
Early aged, and often cold,
Sparrows unnoticed by the Father;
Lambs for whom time had not a fold.

161. Sleeping.

A long, long sleep, a famous sleep
That makes no show for dawn
By stretch of limb or stir of lid,
An independent one.

Was ever idleness like this?
Within a hut of stone
To bask the centuries away
Nor once look up for noon?

162. She Went As Quiet As The Dew

She went as quiet as the dew
From a familiar flower.
Not like the dew did she return
At the accustomed hour!

She dropt as softly as a star
From out my summer's eve;
Less skilful than Leverrier
It's sorer to believe!

163. Secrets.

The skies can't keep their secret!
They tell it to the hills
The hills just tell the orchards
And they the daffodils!

A bird, by chance, that goes that way
Soft overheard the whole.
If I should bribe the little bird,
Who knows but she would tell?

I think I won't, however,
It's finer not to know;
If summer were an axiom,
What sorcery had snow?

So keep your secret, Father!
I would not, if I could,
Know what the sapphire fellows do,
In your new-fashioned world!

164. Returning.

I years had been from home,
And now, before the door,
I dared not open, lest a face
I never saw before

Stare vacant into mine
And ask my business there.
My business,   just a life I left,
Was such still dwelling there?

I fumbled at my nerve,
I scanned the windows near;
The silence like an ocean rolled,
And broke against my ear.

I laughed a wooden laugh
That I could fear a door,
Who danger and the dead had faced,
But never quaked before.

I fitted to the latch
My hand, with trembling care,
Lest back the awful door should spring,
And leave me standing there.

I moved my fingers off
As cautiously as glass,
And held my ears, and like a thief

Fled gasping from the house.

165. Resurrection.

'T was a long parting, but the time
For interview had come;
Before the judgment-seat of God,
The last and second time

These fleshless lovers met,
A heaven in a gaze,
A heaven of heavens, the privilege
Of one another's eyes.

No lifetime set on them,
Apparelled as the new
Unborn, except they had beheld,
Born everlasting now.

Was bridal e'er like this?
A paradise, the host,
And cherubim and seraphim
The most familiar guest.

166. Requiem.

Taken from men this morning,
Carried by men to-day,
Met by the gods with banners
Who marshalled her away.

One little maid from playmates,
One little mind from school,
There must be guests in Eden;
All the rooms are full.

Far as the east from even,
Dim as the border star,
Courtiers quaint, in kingdoms,
Our departed are.

167. Remembrance.

Remembrance has a rear and front,
'T is something like a house;
It has a garret also
For refuse and the mouse,

Besides, the deepest cellar
That ever mason hewed;
Look to it, by its fathoms
Ourselves be not pursued.

168. At Half-Past Three A Single Bird

At half-past three a single bird
Unto a silent sky
Propounded but a single term
Of cautious melody.

At half-past four, experiment
Had subjugated test,
And lo! her silver principle
Supplanted all the rest.

At half-past seven, element
Nor implement was seen,
And place was where the presence was,
Circumference between.

169. Wild Nights! Wild Nights!

Wild nights! Wild nights!
Were I with thee,
Wild nights should be
Our luxury!

Futile the winds
To a heart in port,
Done with the compass,
Done with the chart.

Rowing in Eden!
Ah! the sea!
Might I but moor
To-night in thee!

170. With A Flower-I

I hide myself within my flower,
That wearing on your breast,
You, unsuspecting, wear me too
And angels know the rest.

I hide myself within my flower,
That, fading from your vase,
You, unsuspecting, feel for me
Almost a loneliness.

171. With A Flower-II

When roses cease to bloom, dear,
And violets are done,
When bumble-bees in solemn flight
Have passed beyond the sun,

The hand that paused to gather
Upon this summer's day
Will idle lie, in Auburn,
Then take my flower, pray!

172. Presentiment Is That Long Shadow On The Lawn

Presentiment is that long shadow on the lawn
Indicative that suns go down;
The notice to the startled grass
That darkness is about to pass.

173. Safe In Their Alabaster Chambers

Safe in their alabaster chambers,
Untouched by morning and untouched by noon,
Sleep the meek members of the resurrection,
Rafter of satin, and roof of stone.

Light laughs the breeze in her castle of sunshine;
Babbles the bee in a stolid ear;
Pipe the sweet birds in ignorant cadence,
Ah, what sagacity perished here!

Grand go the years in the crescent above them;
Worlds scoop their arcs, and firmaments row,
Diadems drop and Doges surrender,
Soundless as dots on a disk of snow.

174. So Bashful When I Spied Her

So bashful when I spied her,
So pretty, so ashamed!
So hidden in her leaflets,
Lest anybody find;

So breathless till I passed her,
So helpless when I turned
And bore her, struggling, blushing,
Her simple haunts beyond!

For whom I robbed the dingle,
For whom betrayed the dell,
Many will doubtless ask me,
But I shall never tell!

175. A Tempest.

An awful tempest mashed the air,
The clouds were gaunt and few;
A black, as of a spectre's cloak,
Hid heaven and earth from view.

The creatures chuckled on the roofs
And whistled in the air,
And shook their fists and gnashed their teeth.
And swung their frenzied hair.

The morning lit, the birds arose;
The monster's faded eyes
Turned slowly to his native coast,
And peace was Paradise!

176. A Thought Went Up My Mind To-Day

A thought went up my mind to-day
That I have had before,
But did not finish,   some way back,
I could not fix the year,

Nor where it went, nor why it came
The second time to me,
Nor definitely what it was,
Have I the art to say.

But somewhere in my soul, I know
I 've met the thing before;
It just reminded me   't was all
And came my way no more.

177. Almost!

Within my reach!
I could have touched!
I might have chanced that way!
Soft sauntered through the village,
Sauntered as soft away!
So unsuspected violets
Within the fields lie low,
Too late for striving fingers
That passed, an hour ago.

178. As Imperceptibly As Grief

As imperceptibly as grief
The summer lapsed away,
Too imperceptible, at last,
To seem like perfidy.

A quietness distilled,
As twilight long begun,
Or Nature, spending with herself
Sequestered afternoon.

The dusk drew earlier in,
The morning foreign shone,
A courteous, yet harrowing grace,
As guest who would be gone.

And thus, without a wing,
Or service of a keel,
Our summer made her light escape
Into the beautiful.

179. Simplicity.

How happy is the little stone
That rambles in the road alone,
And does n't care about careers,
And exigencies never fears;
Whose coat of elemental brown
A passing universe put on;
And independent as the sun,
Associates or glows alone,
Fulfilling absolute decree
In casual simplicity.

180. The Coming Of Night

How the old mountains drip with sunset,
And the brake of dun!
How the hemlocks are tipped in tinsel
By the wizard sun!

How the old steeples hand the scarlet,
Till the ball is full,
Have I the lip of the flamingo
That I dare to tell?

Then, how the fire ebbs like billows,
Touching all the grass
With a departing, sapphire feature,
As if a duchess pass!

How a small dusk crawls on the village
Till the houses blot;
And the odd flambeaux no men carry
Glimmer on the spot!

Now it is night in nest and kennel,
And where was the wood,
Just a dome of abyss is nodding
Into solitude!

These are the visions baffled Guido;
Titian never told;
Domenichino dropped the pencil,

Powerless to unfold.

181. The Snow

It sifts from leaden sieves,
It powders all the wood,
It fills with alabaster wool
The wrinkles of the road.

It makes an even face
Of mountain and of plain,
Unbroken forehead from the east
Unto the east again.

It reaches to the fence,
It wraps it, rail by rail,
Till it is lost in fleeces;
It flings a crystal veil

On stump and stack and stem,
The summer's empty room,
Acres of seams where harvests were,
Recordless, but for them.

It ruffles wrists of posts,
As ankles of a queen,
Then stills its artisans like ghosts,
Denying they have been.

182. With Flowers–I

South winds jostle them,
Bumblebees come,
Hover, hesitate,
Drink, and are gone.

Butterflies pause
On their passage Cashmere;
I, softly plucking,
Present them here!

183. With Flowers-II

If recollecting were forgetting,
Then I remember not;
And if forgetting, recollecting,
How near I had forgot!
And if to miss were merry,
And if to mourn were gay,
How very blithe the fingers
That gathered these to-day!

184. Who?

My friend must be a bird,
Because it flies!
Mortal my friend must be,
Because it dies!
Barbs has it, like a bee.
Ah, curious friend,
Thou puzzlest me!

185. When I Hoped I Feared

When I hoped I feared,
Since I hoped I dared;
Everywhere alone
As a church remain;
Spectre cannot harm,
Serpent cannot charm;
He deposes doom,
Who hath suffered him.

186. Water Is Taught By Thirst

Water is taught by thirst;
Land, by the oceans passed;
Transport, by throe;
Peace, by its battles told;
Love, by memorial mould;
Birds, by the snow.

187. Time's Lesson

Mine enemy is growing old,
I have at last revenge.
The palate of the hate departs;
If any would avenge,

Let him be quick, the viand flits,
It is a faded meat.
Anger as soon as fed is dead;
'T is starving makes it fat.

188. The Sleeping Flowers

"Whose are the little beds," I asked,
"Which in the valleys lie?"
Some shook their heads, and others smiled,
And no one made reply.

"Perhaps they did not hear," I said;
"I will inquire again.
Whose are the beds, the tiny beds
So thick upon the plain?"

"'T is daisy in the shortest;
A little farther on,
Nearest the door to wake the first,
Little leontodon.

"'T is iris, sir, and aster,
Anemone and bell,
Batschia in the blanket red,
And chubby daffodil."

Meanwhile at many cradles
Her busy foot she plied,
Humming the quaintest lullaby
That ever rocked a child.

"Hush! Epigea wakens!
The crocus stirs her lids,
Rhodora's cheek is crimson,

She's dreaming of the woods."

Then, turning from them, reverent,
"Their bed-time 't is," she said;
"The bumble-bees will wake them
When April woods are red."

189. The Robin.

The robin is the one
That interrupts the morn
With hurried, few, express reports
When March is scarcely on.

The robin is the one
That overflows the noon
With her cherubic quantity,
An April but begun.

The robin is the one
That speechless from her nest
Submits that home and certainty
And sanctity are best.

190. The Railway Train

I like to see it lap the miles,
And lick the valleys up,
And stop to feed itself at tanks;
And then, prodigious, step

Around a pile of mountains,
And, supercilious, peer
In shanties by the sides of roads;
And then a quarry pare

To fit its sides, and crawl between,
Complaining all the while
In horrid, hooting stanza;
Then chase itself down hill

And neigh like Boanerges;
Then, punctual as a star,
Stop   docile and omnipotent
At its own stable door.

191. The Outlet

My river runs to thee:
Blue sea, wilt welcome me?

My river waits reply.
Oh sea, look graciously!

I'll fetch thee brooks
From spotted nooks,

Say, sea,
Take me!

192. The Only Ghost I Ever Saw

The only ghost I ever saw
Was dressed in mechlin,   so;
He wore no sandal on his foot,
And stepped like flakes of snow.
His gait was soundless, like the bird,
But rapid, like the roe;
His fashions quaint, mosaic,
Or, haply, mistletoe.

His conversation seldom,
His laughter like the breeze
That dies away in dimples
Among the pensive trees.
Our interview was transient,
Of me, himself was shy;
And God forbid I look behind
Since that appalling day!

193. The Mushroom

The mushroom is the elf of plants,
At evening it is not;
At morning in a truffled hut
It stops upon a spot

As if it tarried always;
And yet its whole career
Is shorter than a snake's delay,
And fleeter than a tare.

'T is vegetation's juggler,
The germ of alibi;
Doth like a bubble antedate,
And like a bubble hie.

I feel as if the grass were pleased
To have it intermit;
The surreptitious scion
Of summer's circumspect.

Had nature any outcast face,
Could she a son contemn,
Had nature an Iscariot,
That mushroom,   it is him.

194. The Journey

Our journey had advanced;
Our feet were almost come
To that odd fork in Being's road,
Eternity by term.

Our pace took sudden awe,
Our feet reluctant led.
Before were cities, but between,
The forest of the dead.

Retreat was out of hope,
Behind, a sealed route,
Eternity's white flag before,
And God at every gate.

195. The Humming-Bird

A route of evanescence
With a revolving wheel;
A resonance of emerald,
A rush of cochineal;
And every blossom on the bush
Adjusts its tumbled head,
The mail from Tunis, probably,
An easy morning's ride.

196. The Forgotten Grave

After a hundred years
Nobody knows the place,
Agony, that enacted there,
Motionless as peace.

Weeds triumphant ranged,
Strangers strolled and spelled
At the lone orthography
Of the elder dead.

Winds of summer fields
Recollect the way,
Instinct picking up the key
Dropped by memory.

197. Why?

The murmur of a bee
A witchcraft yieldeth me.
If any ask me why,
'T were easier to die
Than tell.

The red upon the hill
Taketh away my will;
If anybody sneer,
Take care, for God is here,
That's all.

The breaking of the day
Addeth to my degree;
If any ask me how,
Artist, who drew me so,
Must tell!

198. Who Has Not Found The Heaven Below

Who has not found the heaven below
Will fail of it above.
God's residence is next to mine,
His furniture is love.

199. Where Every Bird Is Bold To Go

Where every bird is bold to go,
And bees abashless play,
The foreigner before he knocks
Must thrust the tears away.

200. We Never Know We Go, When We Are Going

We never know we go, when we are going
We jest and shut the door;
Fate following behind us bolts it,
And we accost no more.